THE TIMOTHY INITIATIVE

Disciples Making Disciples
Level 1

Edited by TTI Staff
4.19.19

2 Timothy 2:2

"And the things you have heard from me among many witnesses, commit these to faithful men who will be able to teach others also."

TTI Contact Information:

admin@ttionline.org

TTI Website:

www.ttionline.org

DMD Level 1
This edition published by The Timothy Initiative

For information: The Timothy Initiative
2101 Vista Parkway, Suite 201
West Palm Beach, FL 33411

Scripture quotations are from: The New King James Version
Copyright © 1979, 1980, 1982 by Thomas Nelson, Inc.
Used by permission. All rights reserved.

Acknowledgments

We would like to acknowledge and thank the following individuals and ministries for their godly character, leadership, insight, and inspiration which contributed to the formation of this manual:

1. TTI church planters and disciple makers around the world
2. George Patterson and Richard Scoggins' *Church Multiplication Guide*
3. Curtis Sergeant, Ying Kai, and *T4T*
4. Bruce Bennett and One Mission in South Africa for their *Mobilizing Members* manual
5. Campus Crusade's *Prayer, Care, and Share* manual.
6. Dr. Alex Abraham & Operation Agape
7. Joshua Institute in Asia
8. David Watson and *Discovery Bible Study* principles
9. Nathan Shank and *Four Fields of Kingdom Growth*
10. Jimmy Scroggins and Three Circles

Table of Contents

Welcome, Introduction & Mission
Disciples Making Disciples Level 1

What is The Timothy Initiative?

The Timothy Initiative (TTI) is an international disciple making and church planting movement. TTI was established with the purpose to train and multiply disciple makers and church planters around the world.

What is the Mission of TTI?

TTI's mission is to advance Christ's Kingdom by multiplying disciples and disciple making churches around the world.

What is the Vision of TTI?

In obedience to Jesus and through Kingdom partnerships, TTI's vision is to see multiplying disciple making churches in every place and people group.

Brief History of TTI

TTI was originally called "Project India," as India was where we started. It was not until 2009 that we settled on the name The Timothy Initiative. Since then, TTI has expanded across Asia, Africa, and the Americas. Today, TTI has planted tens of thousands of churches across 42 countries and is committed to continue training disciple makers!

TTI's Core Values

1. **Kingdom Focused**...It's all about the King of kings and His Kingdom, so we share the work and give God the credit.

2. **Spirit-Led – Scripture-Based:** The Holy Spirit and The Holy Scriptures are our guides in planting multiplying churches.

3. **Integrity First:** God values integrity... so do we.

4. **Disciple Making Leads to Church Planting:** The best way to plant churches is by making disciple makers.

5. **Prayer is Priority:** We pray throughout the process of planning and planting churches.

6. **People Matter:** All people matter to God, so we reach out to everyone. Large and small tribes, people groups, urban cities, remote villages, rich, poor... everyone!

7. **Faith Driven:** We want to bring glory to God. If there is no faith involved, there is no glory for God.

These core values are very significant to TTI. They are what makes TTI unique, and we encourage you to adopt them to your own life and ministry.

Purpose and Expected Outcomes

The purpose of this manual is to train, mobilize, and multiply disciple makers. In doing so, the Gospel will spread at a fast pace! We believe every believer is a disciple, and every disciple is called to be a disciple maker. It is important to note a few key distinctives as you begin this training.

TTI's working definition of a disciple maker is as follows:

For those who like to simplify, a **disciple maker is one who lives like Jesus and leads others to do the same.**

For those who like to amplify, **a disciple maker is one who faithfully follows the Spirit of God, lovingly obeys the Word of God, and intentionally invests in the expansion of the family of God by training others to do the same.**

The training in this manual is designed for the following outcomes:

Chapter 1: Every disciple maker will experience a Spirit-filled life.

Chapter 2: Every disciple maker will share their story of how Jesus changed their life with people where they live, work, study, shop, and play.

Chapter 3: Every disciple maker will make disciples by telling God's Story.

Chapter 4: Every disciple maker will stand firm in the assurance of their salvation and help others do the same.

Chapter 5: Every disciple maker will experience a healthy prayer life in tune with the Holy Spirit.

Chapter 6: Every disciple maker will experience God through daily devotions.

Chapter 7: Every disciple maker will live a life committed to intentional and obedient personal Bible study.

Chapter 8: Every disciple maker will experience and share with others the blessings of God as Heavenly Father.

Chapter 9: Every disciple maker will be part of a local body of believers committed to the purposes of Christ and His Church.

Basic Terminology for Level 1

- **Training Center:** location where training, learning, and planning takes place (usually in a church building or home).

- **Paul:** primary trainer and mentor. Pauls model pastoral skills while working with Timothys. Pauls intentionally help Timothys make disciples and hold them accountable to follow through to multiple generations.

- **Timothy:** disciple maker and trainer. Timothys are accountable to their Paul and are trained to bring new believers to Christ, disciple them, and lead them to do the same. Timothys intentionally help these new believers (Tituses) make disciples and hold them accountable to follow through to multiple generations.

- **Titus:** new believer and disciple maker in training (disciple of Timothy). Tituses are accountable to Timothys and are trained to become disciple makers.

TTI's Philosophy & Strategy of Training

Philosophy

TTI believes learning and doing go together, and both should lead to training others also. Obedience is a critical part of discipleship...they should not be separated.

With this in mind, all of the training materials produced by TTI are not merely for educational purposes; rather, there is an expectation that every disciple maker will put into practice what they learn in their personal life and ministry. As we partner together under the leading and direction of the Holy Spirit, He will provide each of us with everything we need to bring Him glory and the lost to His Son, Jesus!

TTI partners with churches and leaders to start disciple making Training Centers. Typically, training happens either in existing church buildings or in homes where participants receive hands-on training on how to make disciples of Jesus, who will in turn make more disciples of Jesus. All assignments center on spiritual growth, evangelism, and disciple making. For those interested, *Disciples Making Disciples Level 2* offers additional training on establishing Micro-Churches.

Strategy

We train disciple makers to make disciples where they live, work, study, shop, and play. In this manual, every disciple maker is encouraged to immediately start meeting with and intentionally developing any new believer they lead to Christ. They are also encouraged to target believers they know who are not making disciples.

- The training is Christ-centered and Bible-based.
- The training is relational and non-formal (ongoing mentoring).
- The training is intentional.
- The training is simple and reproducible.

- The training is often local church-based.
- The training is obedience-based and is immediately applicable to the disciple maker's life.

Every Training Should Include

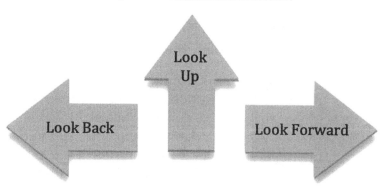

1. **Looking Back** gives everyone a chance to share about and listen to what is happening. It provides an opportunity for encouragement, celebration, and accountability. It also allows challenges to be identified, course corrections to be made, and progress to be measured. Finally, it provides a chance to connect back to the core values, mission, vision, and purpose of the training.

2. **Looking Up** refuels our passion for loving God and others. Spending time in prayer and in God's Word provides nourishment to our souls and inspiration to continue forward. This offers a chance for each disciple maker to continue to learn and grow as Christ-like leaders. Ministry is fueled by our relationship with God. Ownership of the core values, mission, and vision will only happen if we remain connected in relationship with Jesus.

Hearing from God and responding to His word is the primary aim of looking up. After each lesson has been taught, allow some time for prayer and reflection for each person to identify exactly what God is calling them to do. A simple way to do this is to invite God to speak to your heart and ask for Him to show you the areas of greater obedience He is calling you to.

3. **Looking Forward** offers a clear plan of action with timelines and expectations of what to do next. It is important that everyone has clarity regarding what needs to be done before the next training. These next steps are based on what each person hears from God and on the action steps listed in the training. There should be a strong commitment to following through and staying accountable throughout the process. Each trainer should make a note of the commitments made and hold all accountable.

Following the example of Looking Back, Looking Up, and Looking Forward will ensure that every training accomplishes the specific purposes, goals, and outcomes designed.

Chapter 1 Trainer's Guide
The Spirit-Filled Christian Life

 ## Look Back

Review the mission, vision, and core values of TTI.

 ## Look Up

This chapter introduces victorious Christian living...How to live the Spirit-Filled Christian Life. It is critical that you focus on the following as you train through this chapter:

- Begin in complete dependence and recognize that the Spirit of God is the foundation this training must be built upon. With this in mind, train in a way that every disciple maker is depending on the Spirit of God in their everyday life.
- Emphasize how God is always at work, and without the Spirit of God we are powerless and can do nothing.
- **Remember to highlight the expected outcome and key principle!**
- Encourage memorization of key Scripture verses.
- **Hearing from God:** At the end of this chapter allow for a time of silent prayer and reflection, specifically looking for what each person should do in response to God speaking to their heart.

Group Discussion: Focus on the Fruit of the Spirit and connecting to those God is drawing to Jesus. Pray together and listen to what the Spirit of God is saying. Respond in obedience.

Model & Practice: Every trainer should model how they ask the Holy Spirit to fill them and take control of their life each day. Practice together.

 ## Look Forward

Before reviewing the action steps for the week, pause and prayerfully discuss the following questions:

- How is God speaking to your heart today?
- How is God calling you to greater obedience?
- What will you do today & this week in response to God's voice?

*Remember, as you look forward each week, note down what is said so that you may hold others accountable. It is helpful as each person identifies what they are planning to do to begin their statements with "I Will" or "This week I Will _____." Doing this will make the statement more meaningful and the follow-through more measurable. Every trainer should consider keeping an "I Will Journal" or find another practical way to note down the specifics so things are easy to reference from one week to the next.

Action steps for this week:
- Begin each day asking the Holy Spirit to fill you—to take control of your life.
- Memorize *Acts 1:8*.
- As you begin each day in prayer asking to be filled, purposefully look to be connected to people the Father is drawing to Jesus. As names come to mind, begin making a list and commit to praying for them daily (note their names on page 26). When you encounter them, listen to their story and share how God's love has changed your life. Be ready to share what happens!

Chapter 1
The Spirit-Filled Christian Life

Expected Outcome: Every disciple maker will experience a Spirit-filled life.

The Importance of the Holy Spirit for the Disciple

In *John 14*, Jesus promised the Holy Spirit to His disciples.

John 14:16–17 "And I will pray the Father, and He will give you another Helper, that He may abide with you forever—the Spirit of truth, whom the world cannot receive, because it neither sees Him nor knows Him; but you know Him, for He dwells with you and will be in you."

In this passage, we observe how:
- The Father sent the Holy Spirit, at the request of Jesus.
- Jesus described the Holy Spirit as a "Helper" and "the Spirit of truth."
- The Holy Spirit will be with us forever.
- Only followers of Jesus receive the Holy Spirit.

Next, read together *John 16:7-15*.

Take a look at *John 16:7-10*, and notice how Jesus said it is to our advantage that the Holy Spirit comes. Jesus explained that the Holy Spirit will convict the world concerning three areas:
- The world's sin.
- God's righteousness.
- God's coming judgement.

In *John 16:13-15*, Jesus revealed the Holy Spirit will be our guide and will lead us into all truth.

Be Filled With the Spirit

A key verse for the disciple of Jesus is *Ephesians 5:18—* *"And do not get drunk with wine, in which is dissipation; but be filled with the Spirit."*

The phrase, "be filled with the Spirit," is a powerful statement:
- It is a command, not a suggestion.
- It is not something we do ourselves, but something God does.
- It is not a one-time filling. We are called to <u>constantly</u> and <u>consistently</u> be filled with the Holy Spirit.

The indwelling of the Holy Spirit and being filled with the Holy Spirit are not the same thing. The indwelling of the Holy Spirit happens at the point of salvation *(Acts 2:38, Romans 8:9, 1 Corinthians 3:16).* Being filled with the Spirit, as commanded in *Ephesians 5:18,* means to be controlled by the Holy Spirit. We are either being controlled by our sinful desires or by the Holy Spirit (*Romans 8:5-6*).

When we are living under the control of the Holy Spirit, He empowers us to live like Jesus. *Galatians 5:16* tells how **yielding to the Spirit will give us the power to overcome the cravings of sinful desires** (the flesh).

Galatians 5:17-23 identifies both the desires/works of the flesh and the fruit that comes from a life led by and submitted to the Holy Spirit.

Galatians 5:24-25 says that those who belong to Christ have crucified the flesh with its passions and desires and are called to live and walk by the Spirit.

Group Discussion

- How have you experienced the filling of the Holy Spirit in your life this week? What impact has this made in your life?
- Ask yourself; "Is the Holy Spirit producing His fruit in my life? Do I see love, joy, peace, patience, kindness, goodness, faithfulness, gentleness, and self-control in my life?" Explain.
- Share an example of how the Holy Spirit has helped you better understand the truth of Scripture.
- How are you living in line with the Holy Spirit day by day, moment by moment?

Take time for personal reflection and prayer. It is essential that you respond to the Holy Spirit's leading in this before you move to the next section. After taking time to pray individually, pray for one another.

The Holy Spirit in the process of Making Disciples

Jesus discipled His twelve followers for three years. The twelve lived and ministered with their Teacher. Yet, He told them that it was necessary that He go, so He could ask the Father to send the Holy Spirit. He instructed them to wait in Jerusalem for the the promise of the Father—the filling of the Holy Spirit.

Why? *Acts 1:8* says, *"you shall receive power when the Holy Spirit has come upon you; and you shall be witnesses to Me in Jerusalem, and in all Judea and Samaria, and to the end of the earth."*

Jesus promised that His disciples would **receive power** and would **be His witnesses** when they were filled with the Holy Spirit! The same promise is true for every disciple of Jesus today!

Key Principle: God the Father is constantly drawing people to Jesus through the ministry of the Holy

14

Spirit. He <u>invites</u> and <u>expects</u> us to join Him in that process.

 Group Discussion: How does that make you feel? Are you purposefully looking for those people the Father is drawing to Jesus? How do you respond?

As you journey through this training, you will be asked and held accountable to share your story (Chapter 2) and God's story (Chapter 3) with people where you live, work, study, shop, and play. Some of these people will be family, friends, or co-workers. Some will be complete strangers that the Father is drawing to Jesus.

We call these people that the Holy Spirit is drawing to Jesus <u>pre-Christians</u>. They are all around us. The Holy Spirit desires to connect us with them. Are you ready? Are you intentionally looking for them? These people will often be used by God as relational "can-openers" to reaching their friends, relatives, and acquaintances with the Gospel of the Kingdom. Sometimes these catalytic people are referred to as "persons of peace." (See *Luke 10* for this concept.)

Remember, one of the key assignments of the Holy Spirit is to testify about Jesus. As you are filled with Him each day, He will enable you to also bear witness about Jesus. **It is not our strategies or unique gifts that will change the world, it is the fullness of Jesus in and through us!** We must always serve and love out of an overflow of our devotion to Christ as opposed to our own strengh and giftings. Dependence upon the Spirit of God is critical.

Model & Practice: Prayer & The Holy Spirit

 One of the action steps below is to begin each day by asking the Holy Spirit to fill you—to take control of your life.

***You will be seeing this logo throughout this manual. Anytime you see it, your trainer will pause to model and give a chance for you to practice so that you are clear on the principle and ready to transfer it to those you disciple.

Your trainer will now take time to model exactly how to do this, answering any questions you may have so that you can also practice it in your own life.

Take time now to pray together as a group so everyone knows how to do this. Next, divide into smaller groups to practice and hold each other accountable throughout the week. **If you have not already, identify one or two people who can be an accountability partner throughout this training**

Actions Steps for this week

1. Begin each day by asking the Holy Spirit to fill you—to take control of your life. You may need to ask Him to fill you multiple times throughout the day *(1 Thessalonians 5:17-18)*. Note down all you are hearing from God and respond in obedience.

2. Read *Acts 2* every day this week and meditate on the following statement: **Every believer is a disciple, and every disciple is called to be a disciple maker.**

3. Memorize *Acts 1:8*.

4. Ask the Holy Spirit to connect you with a pre-Christian this week and actively pursue identifying who this person is. When He does, share how God's love has changed your life. **Be ready to report back to your trainer who you shared with and what happened.**

5. Under the guidance of the Holy Spirit, begin to make a list of potential pre-Christians (note their names on page 26).

Additional study for this week

Read or listen to the entire Gospel of John.

Make a list of the actions and attributes of Jesus that best reflect who He is. Especially focus on how Jesus taught and interacted with His disciples. Once you have a list, consider your own life and how you measure up next to Jesus who is our model and the standard of perfection. He is the greatest example of who we are called to be like and what we are called to do as we make disciples.

List the various attributes of Jesus that you observed:

_____

_____

_____

_____

_____

Once you have your list, reflect on the following questions:

- As a disciple of Jesus, how should I live?
- Is there anything from Jesus' model of disciple making missing in my life?
- What behaviors, values, and adjustments to the way I spend my time need to change in order to become more like Jesus? Make a list and share that list with someone else.

Chapter Journal

I will: Pray everday and ask Jesus to take control and fill my life.

Notes:

I was finally able to attend the treehouse bible study. I ask God to open up my schedule and I was finally able to attend. I will now strive to attend as many as I can.

Chapter 2 Trainer's Guide
My Story

 ## Look Back

Give everyone a chance to share, hear from others, and be held accountable. Focus on encouragement, celebration, and following through with assignments.

- **Have <u>everyone</u> report about how they followed through with their "I Will" statements and action steps since the last training. Did everyone follow through with what they said they would do?** (This can be done as a large group or in smaller groups.) It is important not to move forward with more training if the previous training has not been put into practice. Intentionally and lovingly hold those you train accountable.
- Sample questions to ask when looking back at Chapter 1:
  - How did inviting the Holy Spirit to fill and control your daily life impact how you lived this week?
  - Can you quote the memory verse – *Acts 1:8*?
  - Were you able to start creating a list of potential pre-Christians that God placed on your mind? How many are currently on your list?
- Review the expected outcome and key principle from Chapter 1. Summarize the key points learned from the previous week.
- Remind everyone that training is for trainers. Everything learned should be put into practice. It should also be trained to the next generation.

 ## Look Up

This chapter focuses on sharing "My Story." It is critical that you focus on the following as you train through this chapter:
- Train in a way that every disciple maker is able to share their personal story of how Jesus changed their life (Each week as you look back, allow time for people to practice sharing their story so they become more comfortable with sharing in front of others).

- Emphasize how every believer is called to be a disciple, and every disciple is called to be a disciple maker.
- **Remember to highlight the expected outcome and key principle!**
- Encourage memorization of key Scripture verses.
- **Hearing from God:** At the end of each chapter, allow for a time of silent prayer and reflection specifically looking for what each person should do in response to God speaking to their heart.

Group Activity: Encourage discussion as you introduce the four types of calls to share the Gospel. Divide into four groups and assign a verse to each group. Let each group report back on their findings.

Model & Practice: Every trainer should demonstrate sharing their story of how Jesus changed their life. Everyone else should also practice writing and telling their story both individually and in small groups. Give everyone a chance to share!

 ## Look Forward

Before reviewing the Action Steps for the week, pause and prayerfully discuss the following questions:
- How is God speaking to your heart today?
- How is God calling you to greater obedience?
- What will you do today in response to God's voice?

Action steps for this week:
- Make a list of all the names God brings to your mind in the places where you live, work, study, shop, and play. Begin praying for each of them daily and look for opportunities to share your story with them.
- Share your story with at least one person from your list this week. Be ready to report back what happens.
- Review the additional study on prayer and fasting. Plan a time for a special day of prayer and fasting. Ask Jesus to help you see others the way that He sees them.

Chapter 2
My Story

Expected Outcome: Every disciple maker will share their story of how Jesus changed their life.

As a Christ follower, you are a child of God and a member of God's family. You can pray directly to, have fellowship with, and spend time with God any time. You are an ambassador for Christ *(2 Corinthians 5:20)*. The Great Commission calls you to spread the Gospel and teach others to obey all of God's ways *(Matthew 28:19-20)*. Every believer, every member of the Body of Christ, is to contribute to the growth and building up of the Church. We are all called to share the Good News of salvation: *the* Gospel!

 Key Principle: Every believer is called to be a disciple, and every disciple is called to be a disciple maker.

There are four types of calls that encourage us to share the Gospel:
1. Call from **Heaven**: The commandment of the Lord Jesus. *"Go into all the world and preach the Good News to all creation." Mark 16:15*
2. Call from **hell**: A rich man's plea to share the Gospel with his family. *"...I beg you therefore, father, that you would send him to my father's house, for I have five brothers, that he may testify to them, lest they also come to this place of torment." Luke 16:27-28*
3. Call from **inside**: Paul was under compulsion to spread the Gospel, motivated by his love for God and the calling God placed on his life: *"I am compelled to preach." 1 Corinthians 9:16-17; Acts 9:16)*.
4. Call from **outside**: Paul heard the call from Macedonia: *"Come over to Macedonia and help us" (Acts 16:9)*. His passion for reaching the lost compelled him to go.

Group Discussion: What do these verses have in common?

Every Christ follower should listen to the calls in their life and respond to the leading and conviction of God immediately.

Imagine there is a disease that is incurable, and many people are dying daily. You repeatedly hear news about the hopelessness of this disease. Now, imagine that someone developed a cure for this disease and chose not to give it to everyone. What will the affected and infected people think of this person? **How would they feel if they knew healing was available but could not access the cure?** Thank God we have the Cure! It is Jesus!

We should not only lead people to become Christ followers but also to become disciple makers. In this way, you can rapidly spread the Gospel. However, most Christians think it is the job of professional ministers (for example the Evangelist, Pastor, Missionary) to proclaim the Gospel. Most Christians consider "evangelism" to be inviting people to church, hoping the pastor will lead them to give their lives to Christ. **This is not God's design! Every Christ follower should regularly experience the immense joy of sharing the love of God with others!** Bringing others to Jesus is the call of every disciple! Every member of the Body of Christ is a minister!

Consider the verse that The Timothy Initiative gets its name from. *"And the things that you have heard from me among many witnesses, commit these to faithful men who will be able to teach others also." 2 Timothy 2:2*

Every Christ follower can and should share their story with their neighbors, friends, family, and network of relationships. God always honors obedience and faithfulness to His Word.

 Group Discussion: Why do you think people do not share their stories of how Jesus changed their life?

Most Christians do not share their story or the Gospel for a few main reasons:

1. **They are afraid!** The One with all authority in Heaven and on Earth is with us and promises never to leave us as we make disciples in obedience to His command (*Matthew 28:19-20*).

2. **They do not sense the urgency of sharing the Gospel.** Across the world, nearly one person every second is dying without knowing the possibility of eternal life in Jesus *(John 4:21-38)*.

3. **They do not see people the way that Jesus sees them.** Their love for Jesus has not compelled their hearts enough to love others and to see people the way Jesus does *(Matthew 9:36; 1 Corinthians 9:16-17; 2 Corinthians, 5:14)*. You may also feel like you do not know whom to share with. Taking the time to consider who needs to hear the Gospel is a simple but important task. In the next few pages you will have a chance to consider whom you can share with.

4. **They do not know how to share the Gospel.** If this describes you, begin by asking the Holy Spirit to empower you to love God, to love others, and to lead and guide your life and ministry *(Romans 8:9-11; Ephesians 3:16, 5:18; Galatians 5:16)*. Some of the best people to share the Gospel with are people you see on a regular basis and have a personal relationship with already.

 Group Discussion: Before moving on, identify the reasons you do not share your story.

The Basic Form of a Testimony

For those who do not know how or do not feel comfortable sharing their story, learning the basic form of a testimony can be a great help. To begin with, it is important to show genuine interest and concern for others. Pray for them and care for them. How often do you pray for others? If you are not praying for others consistently, consider starting now. If you do not care for others, consider starting now. If those you share your story with do not feel like you care for them, they will likely not care to hear from you.

When you do share your story, focus on **three parts** (In *Acts 22 & 26* the Apostle Paul followed this format):

1. **Before Knowing Christ**: How I lived and what my life was like before I believed in Jesus (If you came to Jesus at an early age, start with how Jesus found you).

2. **Knowing Christ**: How Jesus found me (Or how I recommitted or rededicated to an earlier decision).

3. **After Knowing Christ**: How my life has changed because of Jesus.

The ultimate message: "Knowing Jesus as Lord and Savior changed my life!"

Model & Practice: Sharing Your Story
Group Activity:
Practice by writing your own story using the outline on the next page. Focus on how you came to put your faith and hope in Christ. Your trainer will model first exactly how to do this.

- After your trainer models how they share their story, begin writing and telling yours. Adjust it until it is clear and easy to understand.

- Break into small groups and practice telling your stories to one another. Ask for feedback. Adjust accordingly.

- Repeat this process until everyone is clear and confident.

- Finally, let each person practice sharing in front of the entire group.

*Once you finish practicing, write down the best version of your story.

Sharing your story is one of the most important tools in evangelism and is required as you go forward in this training.

*As you begin each chapter for the rest of this manual, you will be reminded to share your story. In fact, it is so important that we recommend before each training session you select 1-2 people to practice sharing their story.

My Story

My life before Christ: (Struggles, brokenness, idols, etc.)

How I came to know Christ: (How Jesus found me.)

My life after coming to Christ has changed! (Church involvement, evangelism, healing, church planting, etc.) *Knowing Jesus as my Lord and Savior has changed my life (list the ways):*

Assignment: Remember the story of the incurable disease and the person who found the cure? The cure to all of life's problems is found in Jesus.

Who needs the cure? List the names of all family members, relatives, neighbors, friends, colleagues, classmates, and any others God brings to your mind who have not come to Christ.

My List I commit to praying for daily and sharing my story:

1. Matesus
2. Dylan
3. Mitchel
4. Brenton
5. Bobby
6. Belle
7. Natalie
8. Bella
9. Jake C
10. Amber
11. MoM
12. Dad
13.
14.
15.

16.
17.
18.
19.
20.
21.
22.
23.
24.
25.
26.
27.
28.
29.
30.

*Important Note: Feedback from TTI disciple makers around the world reveals the average person will have to share their story with 15-30 people for one person to receive Christ.

Do not be discouraged as you work through your list if a large percentage do not respond positively! Your job as a disciple and ambassador is to share what God has done in your life. Don't give up! Continue to pray for them and follow the leading of the Holy Spirit.

If you are struggling to think of 30 names, consider the categories below. If you are not sure if they are a Christ follower, include their name.

List the first people the Holy Spirit brings to your mind:

List people where you live (family & neighborhood):

List people where you work or study (employment & school):

List people where you shop (grocery store, restaurants, coffee shops):

List people where you play (gym, sports leagues, teams, clubs, etc.):

Action steps for this week

Now that you have prepared your story, go, listen, and tell! Take steps of faith! Ask for His passion to reach the lost. Ask the Holy Spirit to also lead you to pre-Christians.

During the week – share your story with at least one person from the list of names you identified above (and any other pre-Christians you encounter). Be ready to report back to your trainer whom you shared your story with and what happened.

Coordinate with your accountability partner your plans, including who, when, where, and how you will share your story this week (understanding it may not always work out perfectly according to your plans). Hold each other accountable, and if helpful, go together to support one another.

*Important Note: You may have opportunities to share your story with people who are not on your list. As you pray, ask God to direct you to those who are hungry for Him and open to His Son, Jesus. He may allow your path to cross with Persons of Peace not listed above.

Additional study for this week

Prayer & Fasting

For those not familiar, fasting is simply choosing to go without food with a spiritual purpose in mind. It is not self-deprivation, but a spiritual discipline for seeking more of God! While fasting, make sure not to allow your cravings to distract but to serve as a reminder for your need for more of Him (*John 4:31-38*)!

Continue praying and begin fasting for the people on your list and for those you happen to encounter. Ask God to give you boldness, wisdom, discernment, and strength to help you be faithful. Ask Him to fill you with His love for the people you will be speaking with this week. Finally, ask the Holy Spirit to open the hearts of the people around you and draw them to Christ.

- Keep a journal of your prayers and also note how God answers them!

Do you know how to ask people if you can pray for them? The following offers three practical ways to ask people how you can pray for them. Remember to follow through and actually pray.

- "I have been praying for you recently, and I was wondering if there is anything specific in your life I can pray for?"
- "I really enjoy praying for people. Is there anything in your life that I may be praying for?"
- Having listened to their story, ask: "Can I pray for you right now?" (in a place that is quiet).

Chapter Journal

I will: _____

_____

_____

_____

Notes:

_____

_____

_____

_____

_____

_____

_____

_____

_____

_____

_____

_____

_____

_____

_____

_____

_____

_____

_____

_____

_____

_____

_____

_____

_____

_____

Chapter 3 Trainer's Guide
God's Story

 ## Look Back

Give everyone a chance to share, hear from others, and be held accountable. Focus on encouragement, celebration, and following through with assignments.

- Have <u>everyone</u> report back on how they shared their story and followed through with what they said they would do since the last training. (This can be done as a large group or in smaller groups). Remember: Intentionally and lovingly hold those you train accountable.
  - If some or many did not follow through with sharing their story, consider not moving on with a new lesson and instead spend time in prayer, practicing, and planning, specifically identifying how each person will share their story this week.
- Review the expected outcome and key principle from Chapter 2. Summarize the key points learned from the previous week.
- Remind everyone that training is for trainers. Are they training others with what they are learning? Has anyone trained someone else how to share their story?

Before Looking Up have at least 2 people practice sharing their story in front of the group. Repeat this process at every future training until everyone becomes extremely comfortable.

 ## Look Up

This chapter focuses on sharing "God's Story." It is critical that you focus on the following as you train through this chapter:

- Train in a way that every disciple maker is able to share the Gospel by telling God's story using the two methods introduced (3 Circles & the Bridge Illustration).
- Emphasize the importance of listening to and caring for others. If you do not listen to others, they will not listen to you.

- **Remember to highlight the expected outcome and key principle!**
- Encourage memorization of key Scripture verses.
- **Hearing from God:** At the end of this chapter, allow for a time of silent prayer and reflection, specifically looking for what each person should do in response to God speaking to their heart.

Group Activity: Each person should practice sharing God's Story until they are comfortable and confident (ideally in 2-3 minutes)! Do not move on until everyone can share their story and God's story confidently and naturally using 3 Circles or the Bridge Illustration.

Model & Practice: Every trainer should present the Gospel by sharing God's Story using 3 Circles and the Bridge Illustration.

 ## Look Forward

Before reviewing the Action Steps for the week, pause and prayerfully discuss the following questions:
- How is God speaking to your heart today?
- How is God calling you to greater obedience?
- What will you do today & this week in response to God's voice?

Action steps for this week:
- Continue praying daily for the people on your list.
- Share your story or God's story with at least 2 people from your list this week. Try to use 3 Circles or the Bridge Illustration when you can. Be ready to report back to your trainer what happens!
- Begin memorizing all of the verses used in the Bridge Illustration.

Chapter 3
God's Story

Expected Outcome: Every disciple maker will make disciples by telling God's Story.

In the previous chapter we looked at how to tell **Your Story**. In this chapter, we will learn and practice telling **God's Story**. While there are many ways to tell God's story, we are going to practice using a method called *3 Circles*. There are numerous variations to this approach, and you can adapt it as you see fit. The main goal is to actively and intentionally share God's Story with others.

 Key Principle: God loved the world so much that He sent His Son Jesus, so that those who believe in Him will receive eternal life (*John 3:16*).

3 Circles Model

GOD'S DESIGN — SIN → BROKENNESS

GO

RESTORED

TURN & BELIEVE

JESUS

Sharing God's story is about having a conversation that centers on the love of God and His love for others. Think for a moment how often you have conversations where people share problems or challenges they are facing.

Using *3 Circles* can help you turn everyday conversations about problems and challenges people are having into conversations about Jesus and the Gospel. It does not always happen this way, but God's Story conversations often stem from listening to other people's stories first. **This is important because understanding and identifying where people are hurting or struggling is a great way to start the conversation.**

There are many ways people will go about sharing their fears, anxiety, brokenness, or emptiness. As you listen, look for an opportunity to pray for them and ask them if you can show them a picture that changed your life. If they say yes, begin drawing 3 Circles.

 Group Discussion: Talk together about some of the common ways people share their brokenness and challenges in everyday conversations.

 Circle 1: Brokenness

Most people don't need to be convinced that the world is broken *(Romans 3:10)*. Both personal and worldwide brokenness surrounds us. As you listen to the trials others are going through, it is important to try to identify what they have done to avoid, escape, or get relief from the problems they identified. Eventually, everything people do to avoid, escape, or find relief from their brokenness will lead back to an awareness of brokenness and emptiness *(Colossians 1:21)*.

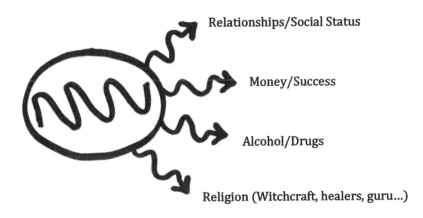

Relationships/Social Status

Money/Success

Alcohol/Drugs

Religion (Witchcraft, healers, guru...)

Keep in Mind: People often use relationships or substances to find healing for brokenness. They may pursue education, work, success, or money as a way to escape from life's problems. They may even try religion or modifying their behavior in an attempt to fix things.

The point here is to listen to their story and relate the circle that symbolizes brokenness to them (or you can share your story and how you tried to deal with your own brokenness). Draw a picture based on the ways they have tried to deal with their own brokenness. This lets them know you are listening. The lines coming out of brokenness show the ways they have tried to deal with their problems in life visually (they are like elastic cords...no matter how far away you try to get from brokenness you will always end up back where you started...If they have not shared their story, you can share how you previously attempted to deal with your brokenness.)

Jesus died for our sins and wants to set people free and forgive them. Brokenness and emptiness are a result of sin. Try to identify the ways people have tried to deal with their brokenness and emptiness through their own efforts (*Romans 1:24-25*).

Circle 2: God's Perfect Design

The second circle to draw represents God's heart and perfect design. We want to share that brokenness was never God's heart or part of His perfect design. You can ask them, "Do you know what God's heart was?" or "Do you know what God's perfect design was?" They may suggest it is changing our behaviors, going to church, being good, or maybe they will not know.

God's heart for everyone is a relationship. When life was lived according to His design, it was perfect (*Genesis 1:26-27, 31*). There was no death, disease, worry, fear, or anxiety... but we were tricked into thinking that we could be like God or there was something better than God's design for us.

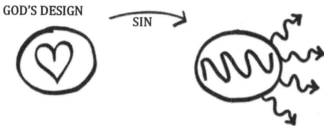

So, we abandoned God. That's when sin entered the world. Sin is anything against God's perfect design. As a result of sin, we became broken and empty. (Draw a line from "God's Design" to "Brokenness" and label it "Sin.")

Bad News! This left us with no way to get back to a love relationship with God and His perfect design.

Good News! When we couldn't get back to God, God came to us.

<u>Circle 3: Jesus</u>
The third circle represents Jesus!

 God sent His son Jesus **down** (draw a down arrow) into our brokenness to die on a **cross** (draw a cross) for our sins (*John 3:16*). He lived a sinless life and offered His life as a sacrifice for ours. Jesus became broken, humbled Himself, and became the perfect sacrifice for our sins.

Three days later Jesus **rose** (draw an up arrow) from the dead so that we could be restored into a right relationship with God and back to His perfect design (*1 Corinthians 15:4*).

What is our response to Jesus?

Jesus tells us to do two things: **Turn** (repent) from our sins and **Believe** in Him as the Lord and Savior of our lives *(Romans 10:9-10)*. When we turn and believe in Jesus, we submit to Him as King. (Draw a crown on the "Jesus" circle: He is the King!)

Jesus tells us to leave the sin, brokenness, and emptiness behind and promises to turn our brokenness into a new creation (*2 Corinthians 5:17*). Jesus forgives us of our sins and sets us free from our brokenness and separation from God. Sin no longer has power over our lives as we are given a new identity and receive the righteousness of God through

Jesus *(2 Corinthians 5:21)*. (Draw an arrow from "Brokenness" to "Jesus" and label it "Turn & Believe.")

Jesus **restored** us to a right relationship with God, so we have the opportunity to receive God's love and grow in our relationship with Him *(2 Corinthians 5:17-18)*. (Draw an arrow from "Jesus" to "God's Design" and label it "Restored.")

With this in mind, Jesus tells us to GO back into a world that is broken and empty and share with others the love, hope, and healing found only in Him, so they can turn from their sin and brokenness into a love relationship with God *(Colossians 1:22-23)*. We now have the ability, through the empowerment of the Holy Spirit, to live a life free from the bondage of sin. This is the hope we have in Jesus and is the hope that others desperately need to experience for themselves. (Draw a dotted line from "God's Design" to "Brokenness" and label it "Go.")

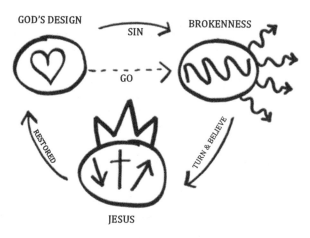

No matter how broken our lives are, there is hope for everyone! **When you get to this point in sharing God's story, ask if there is anything that is stopping them from making Jesus the King of their life today.**

After you share your story or the Gospel in any form, you can ask, "Would you like to make Jesus King of your life now?" If they say yes, lead the person to the Lord immediately. You can use the simple prayer below as an example. Remember there is nothing special about reciting the words below...it is through faith in Christ that we are saved (*Ephesians 2:8-9*).

Lord Jesus, I confess that I am a sinner. I am sorry for all the wrong things I have done in my life. I believe and place my faith in YOU, that YOU came to this world, lived a perfect life, and died for my sins, were raised to life again and through YOU, there is forgiveness of sins.

Jesus, I accept you as my Lord and Savior now. Please come into my life. I am Yours! Thank you for accepting me. In Jesus name, Amen.

After leading someone in this prayer, encourage them to go and share what has happened with their friends and family. It is important to remember that we are not only called to share a Gospel of forgiveness but of Kingdom-living *(Matthew 28:18-20)*. Jesus is our King! We willingly give up everything we have to follow Him! This is a new way of living. Begin meeting regularly with those who make Jesus King of their life. Help them become a disciple who makes disciples.

 Group Discussion: As you consider the 3 Circles presentation of the Gospel, discuss as a group the following four questions.

- Why do I need to be saved?
- Why did Jesus have to die?
- What do I need to do to be saved?
- What happens when I am saved?

Model & Practice: Sharing God's Story

Your trainer will now take time to model exactly how to share God's story, answering any questions you may have so you can confidently share as well.

Group Activity:
Gather in groups of two or three and practice sharing/drawing God's Story. Offer constructive feedback to each other. Make sure it is brief and to-the-point.

- Personalize the lines out of brokenness based on your story or the person's story you are listening to.
- Remove any religious or spiritual terms that people may not understand.
- Adjust the story according to feedback until it is clear and easy to understand.

Repeat this process until everyone is clear and confident.

* Alternative Option for Sharing God's Story *

As mentioned above, there are a variety of ways to share the Gospel and we want to offer an alternative and simplified version of God's Story. Whatever is easier for you we recommend using. **The main point is to introduce people to Jesus!**

The following method of sharing God's Story is known as the Bridge illustration or the Romans Road and uses another simple drawing. This is something you can draw as you share God's Story.

Begin by **drawing the following picture**:

Explain the gap is man's separation from God.

1. ***Romans 3:23:*** *"All have sinned, and have fallen short of the glory of God."*

To sin means to miss the mark. If you try to throw a rock over a mountain, the attempt will fall short. Some will throw farther than others, but all will fall short.

2. ***Romans 6:23:*** *"The payment of sin is death, but the free gift of God is eternal life through Jesus Christ our Lord."*

What we earn for being a sinner is death. What we receive from God, as a free gift, is eternal life.

Draw a cross to cover the gap.

MAN   GOD

3. **Romans 5:8:** *"While we were yet sinners, Christ died for us."*

This means that Jesus took the separation from God that we deserve. It also means that He did not ask us to fix or clean ourselves up first in order to deserve eternal life. While we were sinners, Jesus died in our place.

4. **Romans 10:9:** *"If you confess with your mouth Jesus as Lord, and believe in your heart that God raised Him from the dead, you will be saved."*

To believe means to depend upon. When you sit down on a chair you depend on it to hold your weight. When we depend on Jesus, we trust Him to do for us what He says He will do. When we trust that Jesus died in our place, we are depending on Him to carry the weight of our sin.

5. **Romans 10:13:** *"whoever calls upon the name of the Lord shall be saved."*

The Bible promises that those who seek after Jesus and call upon His name for salvation will be saved. Commit these five verses to memory as a helpful aid to remembering the path to salvation.

| Romans 3:23 | Romans 6:23 | Romans 5:8 | Romans 10:9-10 | Romans 10:13 |

As people begin placing their faith in Christ, encourage them to immediately begin sharing their story! It is also important to lead them into a closer relationship with Jesus. Begin discipling them immediately!

It is good to follow every Gospel presentation with an invitation to accept Christ *(Romans 10:13)*. After you share your story or the Gospel in any form, you can ask, "Would you like to make Jesus King of your life now?" If they say yes, lead the person to the Lord immediately. You can use the simple prayer below as an example. Remember there is nothing special about reciting the words below...it is through faith in Christ that we are saved (*Ephesians 2:8-9*).

Lord Jesus, I confess that I am a sinner. I am sorry for all the wrong things I have done in my life. I believe and place my faith in YOU, that YOU came to this world, lived a perfect life, and died for my sins, were raised to life again and through YOU, there is forgiveness of sins.

Jesus, I accept you as my Lord and Savior now. Please come into my life. I am Yours! Thank you for accepting me. In Jesus name, Amen.

Model & Practice: Sharing God's Story
Your trainer will now take time to model exactly how to share God's story using the Bridge Illustration, answering any questions you may have so you can confidently share as well.

Group Activity:
Gather in groups of two or three, and practice sharing/drawing God's Story using the Bridge Illustration.

Offer constructive feedback to each other.

Make sure it is brief and to the point.
- Remove any religious or spiritual terms that people may not understand.
- Adjust the story according to feedback until it is clear and easy to understand.

Repeat this process until everyone is clear and confident.

<u>**Action steps for this week**</u>

1. Continue praying daily for the people on your list.

2. Begin memorizing the 5 verses in the Bridge Illustration.

3. Share God's story with 2-3 people from your list this week. Try to use 3 Circles or the Bridge Illustration when possible. **Be sure to report back to your trainer what happens!**

Additional study for this week

Meditate on what you should always be ready to do based on *1 Peter 3:15-16*, *"But sanctify the Lord God in your hearts, and always be ready to give a defense to everyone who asks you a reason for the hope that is in you, with meekness and fear; having a good conscience, that when they defame you as evildoers, those who revile your good conduct in Christ may be ashamed."*

- As you reflect on this passage, what preparations must you make to be ready this week?
- Look at *1 Corinthians 2:1-5* and notice what was not included in Paul's testimony: *"And I, brethren, when I came to you, **did not come with excellence of speech or of wisdom** declaring to you the testimony of God. For I determined not to know anything among you except Jesus Christ and Him crucified. I was with you in weakness, in fear, and in much trembling. And my speech and my preaching were not with persuasive words of human wisdom, but in demonstration of the Spirit and of power, that your faith should not be in the wisdom of men but in the power of God."*
- What power was he referring to in verses 4-5? How does that look today in your story?

As you identify people that express an interest in spiritual conversations, try focusing more on connecting them with God...as opposed to a set of ideas or truths about God, a church, or anything else.

Additional Resources:
Free apps/websites that help you share God's Story

3 Circles
lifeonmissionbook.com/conversation-guide

The Story
thestoryfilm.com

The God Test
thegodtest.org

Jesus Film
jesusfilm.org/app

God Tools
godtoolsapp.com

Share Your Faith
howtoshareyourfaith.com

Peace With God
peacewithgod.net

Bible.is
bible.is

Romans Road of Salvation
teenmissions.org/resources/roman-road-to-salvation/

Dare 2 Share
dare2share.org

Chapter Journal

I will: _____

_____

_____

_____

Notes:

_____

_____

_____

_____

_____

_____

_____

_____

_____

_____

_____

_____

_____

_____

_____

_____

_____

_____

_____

_____

_____

_____

_____

_____

_____

Chapter 4 Trainer's Guide
Your Assurance of Salvation

 Look Back

Give everyone a chance to share, hear from others, and be held accountable. Focus on encouragement, celebration, and following through with assignments.

- Have <u>everyone</u> report back on how they shared their story, God's story, and followed through with what they said they would do since the last training (This can be done as a large group or in smaller groups).
- It is important not to move forward with Chapter 4 until everyone has put into practice what they learned in the previous chapter. Remember: Intentionally and lovingly hold those you train accountable.
  - If some or many did not follow through with sharing their story or God's story, do not move forward with a new lesson and instead spend time in prayer, practicing, and planning, specifically identifying how each person will share their story and God's story this week.
- Review the expected outcome and key principle from Chapter 3. Summarize the key points learned from the previous week.
- Remind everyone that training is for trainers.
  - Has anyone identified who they are training yet? An easy tool to use to train others are the simplified lesson plans at the back of this book.

Before Looking Up, have at least 2 people practice sharing their story or God's story in front of the group.

Look Up

This chapter focuses on the assurance we have in our salvation. It is critical that you focus on the following as you train through this chapter:
- Train in a way that every disciple maker is able to stand firm in the assurance of their salvation.

- Remember to highlight the expected outcome and key principle!
- Encourage memorization of key Scripture verses.
- **Hearing from God:** At the end of this chapter, allow for a time of silent prayer and reflection specifically looking for what each person should do in response to God speaking to their heart.

Group Activity: Divide into groups and have each focus on finding Scriptures that answer questions and doubts they have struggled with about their own salvation. Give a chance for anyone who has not done so to make Jesus King of their life.

Model & Practice: Share the most meaningful verse that points to your own assurance of salvation and how it has impacted your life. Ask if anyone is struggling with the assurance of their salvation.

 ## Look Forward

Before reviewing the Action Steps for the week, pause and prayerfully discuss the following questions:
- How is God speaking to your heart today?
- How is God calling you to greater obedience?
- What will you do today & this week in response to God's voice?

Action steps for this week:
- Continue praying daily for the people on your list.
- Share your story and God's story with 2 or more people from your list this week. Continue to use 3 Circles or the Bridge Illustration when you can.

Chapter 4
Your Assurance of Salvation

Expected Outcome: Every disciple maker will stand firm in the assurance of their salvation and help others do the same.

As a Christ follower, you are a member of God's family. As a child of God, you have a direct and personal relationship with Him and are joint heirs of His promises *(Romans 8:17).*

Receiving Eternal Life Through Jesus
Read each question and scripture and discuss together.

1. What is the result of sin?

   "For the wages of sin is death, but the gift of God is eternal life in Christ Jesus our Lord." Romans 6:23

2. People try many different ways to find God yet fail, why?

   "For by grace you have been saved through faith, and that not of yourselves; it is the gift of God, not of works, lest anyone should boast." Ephesians 2:8-9

3. How does God bring us to Himself?

   "For Christ also suffered once for sins, the just for the unjust, that He might bring us to God, being put to death in the flesh but made alive by the Spirit..." 1 Peter 3:18

 Group Activity:
Divide into 7 groups. Assign one verse to each group and have someone explain in their own words how we can be sure of our salvation *(1 John 5:11-13; John 5:24; 10:29 17:1-3; Jude 1:24; Romans 8:16; 8:38-39).*

The Way of Salvation

By grace we are saved through faith not works (*Ephesians 2:8-9*). People try many ways to earn this free gift, yet they ultimately fail.

> Has Jesus died for you? ____ Yes   ____ No
> Have you placed your trust in Him to forgive your sins?
> ____ Yes   ____ No

 Key Principle: If you have trusted Jesus to be your Savior and Lord, then you have received eternal life! You are a Kingdom Citizen! Your service to the King starts now (*John 6:40*)!

What does Jesus promise to those who follow Him?

- In *John 10:28*, Jesus promises eternal life to those who follow Him: *"And I give them eternal life, and they shall never perish; neither shall anyone snatch them out of My hand."*

Eternal life does not only mean you will live forever. It means living with God now in His Kingdom.

- As a result, we are able to live a life of holiness, kindness, love, peace, joy, and strength, forever enjoy the fellowship and the blessings of God. We also live to bless others and tell them about the wonderful love of Jesus.

Your response
Do you know you have received eternal life?
_____ Yes   _____ No

Possible Conclusions (circle/highlight one)
- I have become a follower of Christ.
- I haven't become a follower of Christ.
- I still don't know.

Your new identity

2 Corinthians 5:17 says, *"Therefore, if anyone is in Christ, he is a new creation. The old things have passed away; behold, all things have become new."*

The person who is "in Christ" (Christ follower) will be changed. Circle/Highlight the following changes you have experienced:

- Inner peace
- Awareness and conviction of sin
- Awareness of God's love
- Ability to defeat sin
- Peace of having been forgiven
- Desire to connect with God
- Care and love for others
- Passion for prayer and to know God more fully
- Desire to tell others about Jesus

These desires, experiences, and changes in our lifestyle are the result of the Holy Spirit working in our lives. He confirms that we belong to God.

Romans 8:16 says, *"The Spirit Himself bears witness with our spirit that we are children of God."*

The next time you sin, do you risk losing eternal life?

1 John 1:9 tells us, *"If we confess our sins, He is faithful and just to forgive us our sins and to cleanse us from all unrighteousness."*

This means Jesus forgave all of our sins, regardless of when they were committed. If you are a follower of Jesus and you sin, you still have your salvation!

Based on the previous Scriptures, you can joyfully fill in your "spiritual birth certificate."

> I received Jesus into my life to be my Savior. He called me, forgave my sin, took control of my life, and is my Lord. I have become a child of God, and I am a new creation. I have begun a new life.
>
> Signature:
>
> *Date:

Commit the following verses to memory and share this Good News with others so they can experience His love too!

1 John 5:12 "He who has the Son has life; he who does not have the Son of God does not have life."

Romans 8:38–39 "For I am persuaded that neither death nor life, nor angels nor principalities, nor powers, nor things present nor things to come, nor height nor depth, nor any other created thing, shall be able to separate us from the love of God which is in Christ Jesus our Lord."

John 14:6 "I am the way, the truth, and the life, no one comes to the Father except through me."

Model & Practice: Assurance of Salvation

Your trainer will now take time to share important verses and actual examples of answers given in the past to those who struggle with the security of their salvation.

In groups of two or three, discuss which Scriptures from this chapter you would use to respond to each statement below:

- "I can attain salvation through my good deeds."
- "Can I still be forgiven, or even lose my salvation, if I sin after receiving salvation?"
- "Jesus is one of many paths to salvation."
- "There is no way to be sure if we have salvation."
- "Some of my sins may be too great to be forgiven."

Action steps for this week

Memorize your favorite verses that speak about assurance of salvation.

Continue to share your story and God's story with 2-3 people this week. This is great news and it is God's will. He is willing for all to receive salvation. Be ready to share what happens!

Before going to the next section, discuss if anyone is still struggling with the assurance of their salvation. If anyone has not done so, ask if they are ready to make Jesus the King of their life.

Additional study for this week

Commit yourself this week to living out the Great Commission and the Great Commandment in the power of the Holy Spirit. This needs to become the normal way you live as a Christ follower. In doing so, God will be glorified, and the Kingdom of Heaven will expand on earth.

- What is the main point of the Great Commission? *Matthew 28:19-20*

- What is the Great Commandment? *Matthew 22:37-39*

- How is obeying the second part of the Great Commandment a proof of the first part?

- What is the most loving thing you can do for a person who does not have a relationship with Christ?

Chapter Journal

I will: _____

_____

_____

_____

Notes:

_____

_____

_____

_____

_____

_____

_____

_____

_____

_____

_____

_____

_____

_____

_____

_____

_____

_____

_____

_____

_____

_____

_____

Chapter 5 Trainer's Guide
Living a Life of Prayer

 ## Look Back

Give everyone a chance to share, hear from others, and be held accountable. Focus on encouragement, celebration, and following through with assignments.

- **Have <u>everyone</u> report back on how they shared their story, God's story, and followed through with what they said they would do since the last training**
  (This can be done as a large group or in smaller groups).
- It is important not to move forward with Chapter 5 until everyone has put into practice what they learned in the previous chapter. Remember: Intentionally and lovingly hold those you train accountable.
- Review the expected outcome and key principle from Chapter 4. Summarize the key points learned from the previous week.
- Remind everyone that training is for trainers. Are they training others with what they are learning?

Before Looking Up, have at least 2 people practice sharing their story or God's story in front of the group.

 ## Look Up

This chapter introduces how to live a life of prayer and devotion to God. It is critical that you focus on the following as you train through this chapter:

- Train in a way that every disciple maker is able to pray and have personal devotions with God on a daily basis. Encourage everyone to identify a daily time and place.
- Emphasize the importance of spiritual maturity which requires regularly being with God, talking to God, and hearing from God. Especially focus on the model prayer of Jesus from *Matthew 6:8-13.*
- **Remember to highlight the expected outcome and key principle!**

- Encourage memorization of key Scripture verses.
- **Hearing from God:** At the end of this chapter allow for a time of silent prayer and reflection specifically looking for what each person should do in response to God speaking to their heart.

Model & Practice: Every trainer should demonstrate how to use the Lord's Prayer as a model for personal daily prayer time.

 ## Look Forward

Before reviewing the Action Steps for the week, pause and prayerfully discuss the following questions:
- How is God speaking to your heart today?
- How is God calling you to greater obedience?
- What will you do today & this week in response to God's voice?

Action steps for this week:
1. Commit daily to a time of prayer and identify who will hold you accountable. Make sure to choose a specific time and place.
2. Begin praying 7 minutes a day, 7 days a week, for 7 people on your list, intentionally asking God for their salvation. Use the model prayer introduced in *Matthew 6* if you need help.
3. Continue to pray that God will connect you to persons of peace that the Holy Spirit is drawing to Jesus. As He does, share your story and God's story. Try to do so with at least 2-3 people this week.

Chapter 5
Living a Life of Prayer

Expected Outcome: Every disciple maker will experience a healthy prayer life in tune with the Holy Spirit.

Prayer is "talking" with God, "listening" to God, and "hearing" from God. When you pray, you should be authentic and sincere, just as the Bible records how Jesus "talked" with God and taught His disciples.

To really know a person, you need to have regular contact with that person. In the same way, if you want to have a close relationship with God, it is helpful to "set a time" just for God daily.

Why do we need to pray?
1. Prayer is God's command:
   - You should always pray (*Luke 18:1*).
   - Pray in the Spirit, at all times (*Ephesians 6:18*).

2. This is how we show and express our need:
   - You can share all of your anxiety with Him because He cares for you *(1 Peter 5:7)*.

3. To seek God's leading:
   - "*If you call upon Me, I will show you great and mighty things which you do not know*" *(Jeremiah 33:3)*.

4. To receive mery and grace:
   - "*Receive mercy and find grace in your time of need*" *(Hebrews 4:16)*.

What things do you need to pray for?

"Do not be anxious about anything, but in everything by prayer and petition, with thanksgiving, present your requests to God. And the peace of God, which transcends all understanding, will guard your hearts and your minds in Christ Jesus" (Philippians. 4:6-7).

The Content of Prayer

- Praise: Praise God's character and holiness. He is the creator, sustainer, all knowing, all powerful, loving and truthful one (*1 John 1:9*).
- Thanksgiving: Thank God for His grace, mercy, provision, protection, and salvation (*Philippians 4:6-7*).
- Read the Word: Read God's promises in the Bible.
- Pray the Word: Pray through prayers documented in the Bible.
- Ask: Ask God to meet your own needs (*Psalm 135:3*).
- Intercession: Ask God to care for and meet the needs of others (*1 Thessalonians 5:18*).
- Confession: Ask God to forgive your sins (*1 Timothy 2:1*).
- Listen: Ask the Lord to speak to you and respond in obedience.
- Waiting: Be still, allow God to lead your thoughts (*Psalm 100:3*).
- Hearing: Consider the things you have heard from God and from Scripture.

As you seek the Lord in prayer there are always three possible responses from God: Yes, No, or Wait. God does respond: you must be patient! Our only response to God should be obedience.

Keys for Effective Prayer

1. Pray "in Jesus' name" according to the Father's will (*John 14:13*), because only through Jesus can a person come before God (*John 14:6; 16:23*). Praying in Jesus' name is not merely saying the words "in Jesus name," but with a heart in unity with the heart of Christ. **Praying in Jesus' name is also a recognition of Christ's authority.**

2. Ending our prayer with "Amen" means praying with one's true heart (*Matthew 6:13*). Amen means "Let it be so."

3. Pray in a natural and conversational manner; avoid religious babbling (*Matthew 6:5*).

4. One can pray at any time of the day and at any place, sitting, standing, walking, kneeling, lying down, etc. There is no limit on the time, form, and/or place of prayer (*1 Thessalonians 5:17*).

Attitudes of Prayer

Attitude:	Verse:
In faith	*"But when he asks, he must believe and not doubt..." (James 1:6)*
The right motive and reverence	*"You do not have, because you do not ask God. When you ask, you do not receive, because you ask with the wrong motives." (James. 4:2-3, Matthew 6:9)*
Confess sins	*"Wash me thoroughly from my iniquity, and cleanse me from my sin!" (Psalm 51:2)*
According to His will	*"This is the confidence we have in approaching God: that if we ask anything according to His will He hears us." (1 John 5:14)*
Pray with perseverance	*"That...they should always pray and not give up." (Luke 18:1)*

The Model Prayer: *Matthew 6:9-13*

1. Talk to God like a Father (or Daddy)— *Matthew 6:9*

2. Worship and praise Him— *Matthew 6:9*

3. Pray for Jesus to set the world right and return soon— *Matthew 6:10*

4. Focus on advancing His Kingdom and being in line with God's will—*Matthew 6:10*

5. Ask Him to lead and be the King of your life— *Matthew 6:10*

6. Ask Him to meet your needs and those of others you know— *Matthew 6:11*

7. Confess your sins to Him and forgive those you have not forgiven— *Matthew 6:12*

8. Ask Him for protection and victory over temptation and sin— *Matthew 6:13*

Model & Practice: The Lord's Prayer

Your trainer will now take time to model exactly how to pray the Lord's Prayer together with you.

Gather in groups of two or three and practice praying together. Use *Matthew 6:9-13* as your model.

Action steps for this week

Pray—following the model of Jesus—7 minutes a day, 7 days a week, for 7 people on your list. Specifically pray for their salvation and continue to share your story and God's story.

Continue praying for God to connect you with pre-Christians and Persons of Peace. **This is great news and it is God's will.**

He is willing for all to receive salvation. Be ready to report to your trainer next week!

Additional study for this week

Is the impact of the Gospel on your life a private matter, or is it clearly seen and stated?

The Gospel is not something that should remain personal and private. People who keep the Gospel private may know how it relates to their life, but often nobody else does. Their children may never see how the Gospel affects decisions, arguments, finances, etc. Their neighbors may never hear of the hope they have in Christ. Their colleagues are left wondering what makes them different.

How can you make the Gospel and the work of Christ in your life clear to others this week?

Share how your relationship with Christ relates to everything else you do! Talk about Christ! Don't be afraid to point others to Christ! When the Gospel is kept private, it can be quickly lost! Don't let that happen to you!

Chapter Journal

I will: _____
_____
_____
_____

Notes:
_____
_____
_____
_____
_____
_____
_____
_____
_____
_____
_____
_____
_____
_____
_____
_____
_____
_____
_____
_____
_____
_____
_____
_____
_____

Chapter 6 Trainer's Guide
Daily Devotions

 ## Look Back

Give everyone a chance to share, hear from others, and be held accountable. Focus on encouragement, celebration, and following through with assignments.

- **Have <u>everyone</u> report back on how they shared their story, God's story, and followed through with what they said they would do since the last training.**
  (This can be done as a large group or in smaller groups)
- It is important not to move forward with Chapter 6 until everyone has put into practice what they learned about prayer. Remember: Be intentional to lovingly hold those you train accountable.
  - Did you spend at least 7 minutes a day in prayer? Were you able to have a consistent time and place to pray?
  - Did you pray for 7 people on your list every day?
  - Did you specifically pray and take advantage of opportunities to share your story or God's story this week? How did it go?
- Review the expected outcome and key principle from Chapter 5. Summarize the key points learned from the previous week.
- Remind everyone that training is for trainers. You need to be training others what you have learned. Did you train anyone how to pray?

Before Looking Up have at least 2 people practice sharing their story or God's story in front of the group.

 ## Look Up

This chapter introduces the importance of spending time alone with God in order to have a close personal relationship with Him. Some people call this "daily devotions." It is critical that you focus on the following as you train through this chapter:

- Train in a way that every disciple maker is able to pray and have personal devotions with God on a daily basis.
- Emphasize the importance of setting aside a specific time daily to talk with God and spend time in His word. As disciples, we must hear His voice and be ready to immediately obey what He calls you to do.
- **Remember to highlight the expected outcome and key principle!**
- Encourage memorization of key Scripture verses.
- **Hearing from God:** At the end of this chapter, allow for a time of silent prayer and reflection specifically looking for what each person should do in response to God speaking to their heart.

Model & Practice: Every trainer should model how they do their own daily devotions. Encourage those you disciple to practice this week.

 Look Forward

Before reviewing the Action Steps for the week, pause and prayerfully discuss the following questions:
- How is God speaking to your heart today?
- How is God calling you to greater obedience?
- What will you do today & this week in response to God's voice?

Action steps for this week:
1. Commit to a daily devotion and identify who will hold you accountable. Choose a specific time and place if you have not already done so.
2. Continue praying 7 minutes a day, 7 days a week, for 7 people on your list, intentionally asking God for their salvation.
3. Continue to pray that God will connect you to persons of peace that the Holy Spirit is drawing to Jesus. As He does, share your story and God's story. Try to do so with at least 2-3 people this week!

Chapter 6
Daily Devotions

Expected Outcome: Every disciple maker will experience God through daily devotions.

To really know a person, you need to have regular contact with that person. In the same way, if you want to have a close relationship with God, it is helpful to set a time **just for God** each day. Some people call this "daily devotions". **The God of the universe wants to spend time alone with you, every day!**

Two simple parts that identify a devotional life:

1. **Talk with and listen to** God through prayer (based on what you learned in Chapter 5).

2. Let God speak to you by reading and reflecting on the Bible and listening to the Holy Spirit.

The purpose of our devotional life:

1. Worship God – To honor and enjoy Him!

2. Relationship with God – We share our concerns as we draw closer to Him.

3. Be led by God – To obey His will and plans for our lives as we point others towards Him.

The attitude for our devotional time

Read together *Psalm 42:1* and *Psalm 119:147-148* and discuss the attitude the writer had when he wrote these.

Tools for your daily devotions:

Bible: Read or listen to the Scripture every day; then write down or share with someone what you learned from the reading. Reflect throughout the day. The Bible has the answer to four of life's biggest questions. Where do I come from? Why do I exist? How should I live? What happens when I die?

Journal/Notes: You will want to write down what you sense God is saying to you during your devotional time. You can also write down the names and needs of those you are praying for.

Time & Place: Choose a time and place where you can consistently meet with God without being disturbed.

Plan: Read the Bible with intentionality, meditate, record, pray and obey. It is helpful to use a Bible reading plan. You can download an app with various reading plan options at www.youversion.com.

How to Meditate on God's Word:

Meditating on God's Word involves taking the time to ask the right questions over and over. As you read a passage each day, seek to answer the following questions:
- What captured your attention in this passage?
- What did you like about this passage?
- Did anything bother you? Why?
- What did you learn about God?
- What did you learn about people?
- Is there an example to follow?
- Is there a command to obey?
- Is there an action to avoid?
- Is there a promise to claim?
- With whom should you share this truth?

*Important Note: There may not be an answer to each question in every passage. Focus on the answers that apply.

Getting ready to meet with God

Pray:	*Psalm 119:18 "Open my eyes that I may see wonderful things in your law."*
Prepare:	Collect the tools you need and find a quiet place. Prepare your heart to hear from God. Confess your sins.
Meditate:	Carefully read a verse or Scripture portion. Meditate on it. Talk to God.
Obey:	Obey what God reveals to you. Share with others what you have learned.

Developing your Devotional Life

Be faithful in keeping your daily devotions. **Make your time with God a daily priority.**

It is your decision how often you meet with God. If you intentionally seek a daily time with God, you will find that you will grow in your spiritual life.

While Jesus was on this earth He said, *"Seek first His Kingdom and His righteousness" (Matthew 6:33).* Of all the things you could encounter in this world, there is nothing more important than encountering God on a consistent basis. **If you are too busy to spend time with God, you are too busy!**

One of God's desires is for you to have fellowship with Him and to know Him. Your goal should be to praise and worship God.

 Key Principle: The main purpose of daily devotions is to know and worship God and respond in obedience to what His Word and Spirit say.

Model & Practice: Daily Devotions

Your trainer will now take time to model exactly how they do their own daily devotions, answering any questions you may have so that you can also practice it in your own life.

Gather in groups of two or three and discuss how you do your daily devotions and any changes/additions that need to be made based on this chapter.

<u>Action step for this week</u>:

Are you willing to commit to a daily devotion? **Identify who will hold you accountable for your commitment.** Encourage those you disciple to set a specific time and place they will keep a daily devotion. Show them how and hold them accountable to it!

Time:

Place:

*Remember to pray daily for God to lead you to pre-Christians. Also, continue sharing your story and God's story with more people this week. **Be prepared to report the results of your sharing with your trainer!**

Additional study for this week

As you grow in your prayer and devotional life, it is important to recognize that the Christian life is not only about your personal relationship with God, but also about God's plan to save all people. **Being a follower of Jesus involves a lifelong commitment to help others follow Jesus.**

- Read *Psalm 139:13-16* and *Acts 17:24-28.* What theme do you see when you read these verses?

- We must understand that God has uniquely designed, gifted, and placed us in specific networks and relationships so that others may also know Him. Who are you helping to follow Jesus?

- You are not in your family, neighborhood, school, or workplace by mistake. God has uniquely designed you and has placed you exactly where you should be. Are you being obedient? Are you walking in the Spirit? If you don't share Christ with them, who will?

Chapter Journal

I will: _____

_____

_____

_____

Notes:

_____

_____

_____

_____

_____

_____

_____

_____

_____

_____

_____

_____

_____

_____

_____

_____

_____

_____

_____

_____

_____

_____

_____

_____

_____

_____

_____

Chapter 7 Trainer's Guide
Learning to Feed Yourself

 Look Back

Give everyone a chance to share, hear from others, and be held accountable. Focus on encouragement, celebration, and following through with assignments.

- Have <u>everyone</u> report back on how they shared their story, God's story, and followed through with what they said they would do since the last training (This can be done as a large group or in smaller groups).
- It is important not to move forward with Chapter 7 until everyone has put into practice what they learned about daily devotions. Remember: Intentionally and lovingly hold those you train accountable.
  - Were you able to establish a consistent time and place to pray and have devotions? Did you pray for 7 people on your list every day?
  - Did you specifically pray for and take advantage of opportunities to share your story or God's story this week? How did it go?
- Review the expected outcome and key principle from Chapter 6. Summarize the key points learned from the previous week.
- Remind everyone that training is for trainers. Did anyone train someone in daily devotions?

Before Looking Up have at least 2 people practice sharing their story or God's story in front of the group.

 Look Up

This chapter outlines a personal Bible study plan. Focus on the following as you train through this chapter:

- Train in a way that every disciple maker understands the importance of growing in their love and knowledge of God's Word. Make sure they are also able to practically implement a personal Bible study plan.

- Remember to highlight the expected outcome and key principle!
- Encourage memorization of key Scripture verses.
- **Hearing from God:** At the end of this chapter allow for a time of silent prayer and reflection specifically looking for what each person should do in response to God speaking to their heart.

Model & Practice: Every trainer will model how to do a personal Bible study so everyone sees how to do it. Practice together.

 ## Look Forward

Before reviewing the Action Steps for the week, pause and prayerfully discuss the following questions:
- How is God speaking to your heart today?
- How is God calling you to greater obedience?
- What will you do today & this week in response to God's voice?

Action steps for this week:
- Study the Bible using the personal Bible study method at least one time this week in your devotional time. Make sure to follow through on your "I Commit to Statements."
- Continue sharing your story and God's story with at least 2-3 people this week.
- Make sure to also follow up with those you have been sharing with. Encourage anyone you lead to Christ to begin studying Scripture using the same study method.

Chapter 7
Learning to Feed Yourself

Expected Outcome: Every disciple maker will live a life committed to intentional, obedient, and personal Bible study.

A newborn baby relies on his mother to be fed, but he must eventually learn to feed himself. In the same way, Christians must learn to feed themselves in order to mature. The best way to grow is trusting and obeying God's Word and allowing the Holy Spirit to guide us to:
- Study Scripture
- Understand Scripture
- Obey and Apply Scripture
- Communicate Scripture

 Key Principle: Every believer must learn to grow in understanding, trusting, and obeying God's Word.

Knowing and obeying the Bible is a defining element in the life of a disciple. Staying grounded in the Word of God is a critical part of daily devotions and required for ongoing growth and spiritual maturity. We encourage every disciple to read through the entire Bible at least one time per year, every year! **Are you following a Bible reading plan yet?**

Personal Bible Study
A personal Bible study plan is a great way to stay intentional in your study of Scripture and growth as a disciple. The following provides a simple outline to use as you learn to feed yourself from Scripture.

The Plan involves the following steps:

1. Choose a passage of Scripture.
2. Pray for guidance from the Holy Spirit and read or listen to the passage 2-3 times.
3. In your notes or journal divide a paper into four sections.
   - Section One: "Scripture"
   - Section Two: "My Own Words"

- Section Three: "I Commit to..."
- Section Four: "Prayer & Share"

Section 1: Scripture

Copy the passage word-for-word—exactly how it is written in the Bible. When you copy a passage word-for-word, you actually read it aloud several times. This is an effective form of meditating on Scripture! If the passage is too long choose a few of the key verses.

*Important Note: When necessary, you can also use a Bible app or audio Bible to listen and re-listen to the same passage of Scripture.

Section 2: My Own Words

When you finish writing (or listening to) the passage, rewrite (or retell) it in your own words, as if you are explaining it to someone unfamiliar with the context.

When you can clearly communicate to someone else, you know you fully understand. Do not go forward until you can clearly and confidently communicate the passage in your own words.

Section 3: I Commit to...

This section transitions from understanding God's Word to obeying and applying God's Word. Ask the Holy Spirit to reveal things you need to add to your life, take away from your life, or change in your life to obey this passage.

Be specific. What will you do in response? What can you do to obey this passage? Use some of the questions below to help you identify what to do:
- What captured your attention in this passage?
- What did you like about this passage?
- Did anything concern you? Why?
- What did you learn about God?
- What did you learn about people or sin?

- Is there an example to follow?
- Is there a command to obey?
- Is there an action to take or to avoid?
- Is there a promise to claim?
- With whom should you share this truth?

*Try to be as practical as possible, including the action step and who will keep you accountable.

Every time we open God's Word, He invites us into a relationship. **Faith is how we accept His invitation.** God is pleased with those who obey His Word (*John 14:23-24*).

When we study God's Word, we have a choice: we choose to obey Him, or we choose to disobey Him. Your commitment statement is your response to God's invitation.

Section 4: Prayer & Share

 When you finish your study, take time to prayerfully reflect on who needs to hear the truths God has revealed to you. Write down who you can share with. God's Word is not just for you, but for others also! Share with others what you learned and tell them how you obeyed and applied the Scripture to your life. They can also hold you accountable and figure out ways to help you obey God's Word.

You can use the phrase "God taught me something today" and wait for a response. If the Holy Spirit is working in their heart, they will ask to hear more. Share your faith with those who engage in conversation!

Model & Practice: Personal Bible Study

 There are several passages of Scripture for you to practice this method of personal Bible study below.

Your trainer will choose one passage and model how to effectively use this method. After your trainer models, practice together using the template on the next page.

Suggested Passages to Practice

The Shepherd and His Sheep *(John 10:22-30)*
Abiding in Christ *(John 15:1-9)*
The Prodigal Son *(Luke 15:11-24)*
Prayer *(Matthew 6:5-15)*
Fellowship *(Acts 2:41-47)*
Being a Witness *(Acts 1:3-9)*
The Greatest Commandment *(Mark 12:28-34)*
Parable of the Soils *(Matthew 13:3-8, 18-23)*
Parable of the Talents *(Matthew 25:14-30)*
Parable of the Persistent Widow *(Luke 18:2-8)*
Parable of the New and Old *(Luke 5:36-38)*
Cost of Discipleship *(Luke 14:25-33)*
Samaritan Woman at the Well *(John 4:7-45)*
Boldness in the Face of Persecution *(Acts 4:23-31)*

Personal Bible Study Template

Section 1: Scripture	Section 2: My Own Words

Section 3: I Commit to...	Section 4: Prayer & Share

Action steps for this week

1. Study the Bible using the personal Bible study template in your devotional time.

2. Continue sharing your story and God's story with at least two people this week. Make sure to also follow up with those you have been sharing with. **Be ready to report back on what happens.**

Chapter Journal

I will: _____

_____

_____

_____

Notes:

_____

_____

_____

_____

_____

_____

_____

_____

_____

_____

_____

_____

_____

_____

_____

_____

_____

_____

_____

_____

_____

_____

_____

_____

Chapter 8 Trainer's Guide
God Our Heavenly Father

 Look Back

Give everyone a chance to share, hear from others, and be held accountable. Focus on encouragement, celebration, and following through with assignments.

- Have <u>everyone</u> **report back on how they shared their story, God's story, and followed through with what they said they would do since the last training** (This can be done as a large group or in smaller groups).
- It is important not to move forward with Chapter 8 before putting into practice what was taught in the previous chapter. Did everyone practice the personal bible study method? How did it go?
- Review the expected outcome and key principle from Chapter 7. Summarize the key points learned from the previous week.
- Remind everyone that training is for trainers. Are they training others with what they are learning?

Before Looking Up have at least 2 people practice sharing their story or God's story in front of the group.

 Look Up

This chapter highlights how God our Heavenly Father reveals His unconditional love towards His children. He loves, protects, provides and disciplines His children.

- Train in a way that every disciple understands the blessings that come with being unconditionally loved by God our Heavenly Father.
- **Remember to highlight the expected outcome and key principle!**
- Encourage memorization of key Scripture verses.
- **Hearing from God:** At the end of this chapter, allow for a time of silent prayer and reflection specifically looking for what

each person should do in response to God speaking to their heart.

Group Discussion: How does God reveal His love to you? Which aspect of God is most meaningful to you and why?

Model & Practice: Spend some time reflecting on the love of God. As you do, consider the many experiences each person has had sharing their faith with pre-Christians on their list and those that the Holy Spirit is bringing into your life. Pray for one another!

 ## Look Forward

Before reviewing the Action Steps for the week, pause and prayerfully discuss the following questions:
- How is God speaking to your heart today?
- How is God calling you to greater obedience?
- What will you do today & this week in response to God's voice?

Action steps for this week:
- Worship God by praising Him for who He is. Ask Him to search your thoughts, attitudes and relationships. Then repent and turn away from any sins that God reveals.
- Continue sharing your story and God's story with those on your list. Be ready to report back on what happens.
- Memorize *1 John 3:1.*

Chapter 8
God Our Heavenly Father

Expected Outcome: Every disciple maker will experience and share with others the blessings of God as Heavenly Father.

When Jesus taught His disciples to pray, He started with *"Our Father in heaven."* The Bible describes God as our Father. He loves, protects, provides for, and disciplines His children.

 Key Principle: God is your Heavenly Father and loves you unconditionally.

1. The Heavenly Father's Love

Read through the below passages and discuss how God loves you and why God saved you.

Jeremiah 31:3 "The Lord has appeared of old to me, saying: "Yes, I have loved you with an everlasting love; Therefore with lovingkindness I have drawn you."

Romans 5:8 "But God demonstrates His own love toward us, in that while we were still sinners, Christ died for us."

John 3:16 "For God so loved the world that He gave His only begotten Son, that whoever believes in Him should not perish but have everlasting life."

Ephesians 2:4–5 "But God, who is rich in mercy, because of His great love with which He loved us, even when we were dead in our trespasses, made us alive together with Christ."

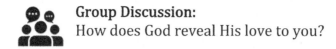

Group Discussion:
How does God reveal His love to you?

In *Luke 15:11-32*, Jesus talks about how a father loved his son. Read through the passage and discuss the similarities there are between this father and God, our Heavenly Father.

2. The Heavenly Father's Protection

Read through the below passages and consider how the Heavenly Father protects you.

2 Thessalonians 3:3 "But the Lord is faithful, who will establish you and guard you from the evil one."

Psalm 34:7 "The angel of the Lord encamps all around those who fear Him, and delivers them."

2 Kings 6:15-18 "And when the servant of the man of God arose early and went out, there was an army, surrounding the city with horses and chariots. And his servant said to him, "Alas, my master! What shall we do?" So he answered, "Do not fear, for those who are with us are more than those who are with them." And Elisha prayed, and said, "Lord, I pray, open his eyes that he may see." Then the Lord opened the eyes of the young man, and he saw. And behold, the mountain was full of horses and chariots of fire all around Elisha. So, when the Syrians came down to him, Elisha prayed to the Lord, and said, "Strike this people, I pray, with blindness." And He struck them with blindness according to the word of Elisha."

1 Corinthians 10:13 "No temptation has overtaken you except such as is common to man; but God is faithful, who will not allow you to be tempted beyond what you are able, but with the temptation will also make the way of escape, that you may be able to bear it."

3. The Heavenly Father's Provision

Read through the below passages and discuss how the Heavenly Father provides.

Philippians 4:19 "And my God shall supply all your need according to His riches in glory by Christ Jesus."

Matthew 6:31-33 "Therefore, do not worry, saying, what shall we eat? or What shall we drink? or What shall we wear? For after all these things the Gentiles seek. For your heavenly Father knows that you need all these things. But seek first the kingdom of God and His righteousness, and all these things shall be added to you."

Romans 8:32 "He who did not spare His Own Son, but delivered Him up for us all, how shall He not with Him also freely give us all things?"

4. The Heavenly Father's Discipline

Read through the below passages and discuss what God expects and how He disciplines His children.

Hebrews 12:6–7 "For whom the Lord loves He chastens, And scourges every son whom He recieves." If you endure chastening, God deals with you as with sons; for what son is there whom a father does not chasten?"

2 Timothy 3:16 "All Scripture is given by inspiration of God, and is profitable for doctrine, for reproof, for correction, for instruction in righteousness."

Group Discussion:
Which aspect of God is most meaningful to you and why?

- His love & kindness
- His provision for your needs
- His discipline and protection
- Knowing His will, character, and nature
- Something else?

Model & Practice: Discussion & Feedback

By now you have had many experiences sharing your faith with those you know, as well as pre-Christians the Holy Spirit is bringing into your life.

Take some time for discussion and feedback as a group to hear what is happening. Based on the feedback, your trainer will focus in on what seems to be the most appropriate topics for discussion.

<u>Action steps for this week</u>

- Identify who you will share with about your Heavenly Father and His love this week.

- Memorize *1 John 3:1.*

- Encourage those you have led to Christ to tell others about the love of God.

- **Report the result back to your trainer.**

Additional study for this week

Worship God and meditate on Him. Focus on the different aspects of His greatness!

- Give thanks to Him for past, present and future blessings.

- Praise God for who He is! (His attributes and names)

- Freely worship and adore Him.

- Ask God to search your thoughts, attitudes, speech and relationships. Confess any sins and be sure to forsake any sins that God reveals.

- Pray for the development of your character and holiness. Pray for ministry opportunities. Reflect on and pray through the Scriptures. What is God saying to you? What must you do in response and obedience?

As you go about your week, share with someone one of the aspects of God that is most meaningful to you.

Chapter Journal

I will: _____

_____

_____

_____

Notes:

_____

_____

_____

_____

_____

_____

_____

_____

_____

_____

_____

_____

_____

_____

_____

_____

_____

_____

_____

_____

_____

_____

_____

_____

_____

_____

Chapter 9 Trainer's Guide
Life in the Church

 ## Look Back

Give everyone a chance to share, hear from others, and be held accountable. Focus on encouragement, celebration, and following through with assignments.

- **Have <u>everyone</u> report back on how they shared their story, God's story, and followed through with what they said they would do since the last training** (This can be done as a large group or in smaller groups).
- It is important not to move forward with Chapter 9 before you have put into practice what was learned in the previous chapter. Can anyone share the memory verse?
- Review the expected outcome and key principle from Chapter 8. Summarize the key points learned from the previous week.
- Remind everyone that training is for trainers. Do those being trained have anyone ready and willing to be trained through this book?

Before Looking Up, have at least 2 people practice sharing their story or God's story in front of the group.

 ## Look Up

This chapter explains the importance of life in the Church. Focus on the following as you train through this chapter:

- Train in a way that every disciple understands as new churches are being planted, the purpose of Christ and His Church should be understood and followed.
- **Remember to highlight the expected outcome and key principle!**
- Encourage memorization of key Scripture verses.
- **Hearing from God:** At the end of this chapter, allow for a time of silent prayer and reflection specifically looking for what each person should do in response to God speaking to their heart.

Group Discussion: Evaluate the 5 fingers and discuss the importance of being connected to a church. Review the privileges and responsibilities of the church.

Model & Practice: Plan a time soon to meet individually with each of those you are training. Together you can assess the growth, development, and discipleship efforts. It is also good to consider what fruit has come from this training and what the plans are going forward. Disciples Making Disciples Level 2 may be an option for some.

 ## Look Forward

Before reviewing the Action Steps for the week, pause and prayerfully discuss the following questions:
- How is God speaking to your heart today?
- How is God calling you to greater obedience?
- What will you do today & this week in response to God's voice?

Action steps for this week:
- Begin meeting together with those you have led to Christ and train them on the importance of life in the local church.
- Obey the command of Jesus in baptism if you have not already. Begin or continue sacrificially giving.
- Continue sharing your story and God's story with at least 2-3 people each week. By now it is becoming part of your lifestyle and is something you can continue without even needing to be reminded. The goal is to get to that point!

Chapter 9
Life in the Church

Expected Outcome: Every disciple maker will be part of a local body of believers committed to the purposes of Christ and His Church.

When you become a Christian, you become a member of God's family. As covered in the last chapter, God is your Heavenly Father and all Christians are your brothers and sisters. We are now part of the same family, *"... the house of God, which is the church of the living God..." 1 Timothy 3:15.*

A household is not a building, and the "Church" is not a place or location of worship; the Church is a body of believers.

 Key Principle: The Church is a spiritual family—with Christ in their midst as King—who love God, love others, and multiply disciples.

Romans 12:5 says that though we are many, we are one body in Christ. *Ephesians 1:22-23* and *5:23* tell how Jesus is over all things as the Head of the Church.

 Group Discussion: How does the Bible describe the relationship between Jesus and Christians?

What is the Purpose of the Church?
Five fingers can help you remember:

 One Finger
The Church has one purpose: To GLORIFY GOD. The Church also has one **Head**—CHRIST.
(*Ephesians 1:22-23, 5:23*).

Christ is the Head of the Church. There is no other. God has ordained only one "Chief Shepherd" (*1 Peter 5:1-4*). Within the body of Christ there is no hierarchy. *"The eye cannot say* to the hand, 'I don't need you." (*1 Corinthians 12:21*). All parts work together for the good of the body. Each believer is a part of the body and membership includes mutual accountability (*1 Corinthians 12:27*).

Two Fingers
The Church has two authorities: The Holy Spirit and Holy Scriptures (Bible).

1. **The Holy Spirit–** God has provided to each believer His Spirit as a counselor (*John 14:26*). The Spirit indwells us at the point of salvation and guides/empowers us toward right thoughts and actions. When we sin, the Spirit brings conviction, leading us toward repentance and confession before God. His voice must be discerned as it guides the believer into God's will. He also empowers the believer for making disciples. He produces spiritual fruit and gives us spiritual gifts which equip us to serve the Church and others towards maturity.

2. **God's Word–** To guide the Church, God ensured the recording of His instruction and plan for mankind. It is without error and is the sufficient tool for discerning all matters of faith and practice. The Scripture speaks to all matters concerning the Church and must be central in the decision-making process of the Body of Christ (*2 Timothy 3:16-17*).

Together, the Spirit of God and the Word of God guide the Church. While the Spirit of God can speak apart from Scripture, there will never be a contradiction to the written Word of God. God's Spirit uses the Word as an instrument to instruct and at times correct the believer. The Word is the Spirit's way of shaping and directing the Church. Together these two provide all that is needed for the Church to move forward in assurance of God's will. (For further study see *Ephesians 5 & Colossians 3.*)

Three Fingers
The Church has three offices and many leaders.

1. Jesus, the Chief Elder/Shepherd (*1 Peter 5:1-4*)

2. Elders/Overseer/Pastor (*1 Timothy 3:1-7, Titus 1:5-9, Acts 14:23, 1 Peter 5:1-4*)
   - Elder is who they are.
   - Overseer/Bishop is what they do.
   - Pastor/Shepherd is how they do it.

3. Deacons/Servants (*Acts 6:3, 1 Timothy 3:8-13*)
   - Deacons serve the Lord by serving the church body.

Qualifications
The qualifications for those who serve and lead a church can be found in *Titus 1* and *1 Timothy 3*.
   - Many believe the pastors are the ones who should do the "work of ministry/service." A more careful reading of *Ephesians 4:11-12* reveals that the works of service are the job of **every** believer.

Four Fingers
The church has four signs of maturity. As a church grows it must take responsibility and ownership of each of these areas:

1. **Self-Governing**: a church is mature enough to make decisions according to its two authorities: Holy Scriptures and Holy Spirit. See *Acts 6:1-7* for an example of this.
2. **Self-Multiplying**: a maturing church understands their role in evangelism and disciple making. Healthy things tend to grow, reproduce, and multiply. Paul encouraged this in *1 Thessalonians 1:7-8*.
3. **Self-Supporting**: a church takes responsibility and ownership for its activities, ministry outreach, and

engagements. See *Acts 2:44-45; 4:34-35* for examples of this.

4. **Self-Correcting**: a proper understanding and application of the authorities in the church will lead to self-correcting behaviors. See *2 Timothy 3:16-17* for examples of this.

 Five Fingers
The church has five functions:

1. **Worship** - the expression of love toward God

   Psalm 149:1 "Praise the LORD! Sing to the LORD a new song, and his praise in the assembly of saints!"

2. **Fellowship** - loving the Body of Christ and bearing one another's burdens

   Hebrews 10:24 "And let us consider one another in order to stir up love and good works..."

3. **Discipleship** – making disciples (including evangelism) and teaching them to obey everything Christ has commanded and ensuring this continues for multiple generations

   Matthew 28:19-20 "Go therefore and make disciples of all the nations, baptizing them in the name of the Father and of the Son and of the Holy Spirit, teaching them to observe all things that I have commanded you; and lo, I am with you always, even to the end of the age."

4. **Ministry** - works of service toward all through actions and attitudes

   Ephesians 4:12 "For the equipping of the saints for the work of ministry, for edifying of the body of Christ..."

5. **Mission & Spirit-Filled Living** – love for God compels our love for others

   Ephesians 5:18-21 "And do not be drunk with wine, in which is dissipation; but be filled with the Spirit..."

   Acts 1:8 "But you shall receive power when the Holy Spirit has come upon you; and you shall be my witnesses in Jerusalem, and in all Judea and Samaria, and to the end of the earth."

We make disciples by going, baptizing, and teaching others to obey ALL that Christ commanded us!

 Group Discussion: Consider the first church in *Acts 2:41-47*. How many of the five functions do you see at work in this body of believers?

Why should we be connected to a local body of believers?
- We need worship, fellowship, discipleship, mutual accountability and encouragement.
- Because of God's command in *Hebrews 10:25 "Not forsaking the assembling of ourselves together, as is the manner of some, but exhorting one another, and so much more as you see the Day approaching."*
- To avoid departing from the truth of the Bible.
- There are mature Christians in church to help us in our walk with Christ.

Privileges and Responsibilities we have in Church:

1. **Baptism is commanded by Jesus and is how we go public with our faith—** *Matthew 28:19-20, Romans 6:1-14, Acts 2:41*

    - Baptism was the starting point of discipleship in the early Church. It is a symbol of our faith, and a critical part of making disciples *(Matthew 28:19-20).*

    - Baptism is a proclamation and confirmation of our faith. Baptism is going public with our faith *(Acts 2:41).*

    - The words and actions of baptism communicate to those present that we are raised to new life in Christ Jesus *(Romans 6:3).*

    - We know and feel that we are freed from the old dead person, and now live a new life in resurrection power *(Romans 6:4–5).*

    - Baptism does not have the power to forgive sin. We are saved when we confess with our mouth and believe in our heart *(Romans 10:9).*

2. **The Lord's Supper (communion) is commanded by Jesus and is how we celebrate and remember His sacrifice.**

    - Jesus personally established communion as a remembrance of His death and shed blood for our sin *(Matthew 26:17-19, 26-30).*

    - When we receive the Lord's Supper, we remember and give thanks *(Isaiah 53:5).*

    - The Lord's Supper is a time to self-examine our actions and faith *(1 Corinthians 11:23-29).*

- The Lord's Supper is a time to pray and reflect on His life, death, and resurrection *(John 15-17)*.

3. **Sacrificial Giving is one way we show love and obedience to Jesus' command to Love God and Love Others.**

   - Giving can include sacrifices of a person's life, goals, time, abilities, and finances.

   - Sacrificial giving is required by God and is a test of the disciple's faith, love, and obedience.

   - God commanded His people in the Old Testament to tithe, telling them the tithe belongs to God. Tithe means 10% *(Leviticus 27:30-31, Malachi 3:8-9)*.

   - Sacrificial giving originates from a thankful and sincere heart. It is motivated by love and given according to what a person has and according to the needs of others. *2 Corinthians 8:9-15*. We cannot worship God without gifts and offerings *(Acts 2:45, 2 Corinthians 9:7)*.

 ## Model & Practice: Growth & Discipleship
Plan out a time to meet individually with your trainer. Together you can assess your growth, development, and discipleship efforts.

It is also good to consider what fruit has come from this training and what the plans need to be made going forward. *Disciples Making Disciples Level 2* may be an option for some.

Action steps for this week

- Follow the command of Jesus in baptism if you have not done so already.

- Begin or continue sacrificial giving.

- Continue sharing your story and God's story to new people this week.

- Begin or continue meeting together with those you have led to Christ and encourage them to join a local body of believers and experience baptism if they have not already done so. For those willing and able, begin training them through this manual.

Chapter Journal

I will: _____

_____

_____

_____

Notes:

_____

_____

_____

_____

_____

_____

_____

_____

_____

_____

_____

_____

_____

_____

_____

_____

_____

_____

_____

_____

_____

_____

_____

_____

Section 1 Conclusion
Spreading the Gospel

As a child of God and a member of God's family, you have assurance of salvation. You can pray directly to God the Father and have fellowship and devotional time with Him at any time. God calls you to spread the Gospel and teach others to obey all of His ways. Those you train must train others about the Good News of salvation *(2 Timothy 2:2)*.

Remember, there are four types of calls to share the Gospel:

1. **The Call from Heaven: the commandment of the Lord Jesus** *(Mark 16:15)*

2. **The Call from Hell: the rich man's plea to share the Gospel with his family** *(Luke 16:27-28)*

3. **The Call from Within: Paul was under compulsion to spread the Gospel** *(2 Corinthians 5:14-15, 18-20)*

4. **The Call from Outside: Paul heard the call from Macedonia to come** *(Acts 16:9)*

Today each Christian should listen to the calls in their life and respond immediately.

We should not only lead people to become Christ followers, but also to become successful "trainers" who train others. A disciple who makes disciples! In this way, you can rapidly spread the Gospel *(2 Timothy 2:2)*.

God's desire is for every Christian to share the Gospel, starting with those close and all the way to the ends of the earth! He will also lead many to plant new churches *(Acts 2:46-47)!*

Consider these 3 blessings:
- It is a great blessing to lead someone to the Lord.
- It is a greater blessing to disciple them and plant a church.
- It is the greatest blessing to help others plant disciple making churches.

Prayerfully consider how God has worked in your life and what He is leading you to do going forward. What changes do you need to make to see it happen?

What's Next?

Now that you have completed *Disciples Making Disciples Level 1*, you have new believers you are investing in to become disciple makers. If you have not already, you must quickly decide how to move this group of new believers into disciples that make disciples.

There are a few ways to go forward in the disciple making relationship.

You can begin gathering with your new believers on a regular basis as a smaller spiritual family under the banner and leadership of your existing church. While you remain aligned to the common vision, mission, and leadership of your existing church, this group of new believers can meet together in homes, offices, clubhouses, coffee shops, barber shops, etc.

- When you gather, we recommend you fellowship, study the Scriptures, pray, and serve both inside and outside the group in the effort to make disciples who make disciples. Remember the 5 functions of the church in Chapter 9.

- We recommend you continue in relationship with your Training Center and begin going through *Disciples Making Disciples Level 2*, which will greatly assist you as you go forward in your discipleship journey and provide a guide and framework for developing your new and growing spiritual family into reproducing disciple makers.

Alternatively, you may choose to continue to disciple your new believers as members of an existing church.

Discipling New Believers

The following pages cover the main points from each chapter of this book. It serves as a field guide to help new believers become disciple makers.

The chapter summaries are a simple model to follow when you meet together. The goals for new believers are a simple way to highlight and track the progress of the disciple making process.

We recommend you frequently meet with your new believers and encourage simple, loving, childlike obedience to Christ! You can also help them immediately identify people in their life they can share the Gospel with (just like you did with them).

Disciple Making Goals for New Believers		
	Yes	Not Yet
Baptism		
Spiritual Fruit		
Understanding Identity in Christ		
Obedience to Scripture		
Spirit Filled Living		
Daily Devotions and "Self-Feeding"		
Comfortable sharing "My Story"		
Comfortable sharing "God's Story"		
Training Others		
Prayer Walking		
Involved in a local Church		
Sacrificial Giving		

Chapter 1– The Spirit-Filled Christian Life

Every disciple maker can experience a Spirit-filled life.

Key Principle: God the Father is constantly drawing people to Jesus through the ministry of the Holy Spirit. He invites and expects us to join Him in that process.

Key Scriptures:

1. **Jesus sent the Holy Spirit for our benefit**— *John 14:16-17*

2. **We are to be filled with the Holy Spirit**— *Ephesians 5:18*

3. **The Holy Spirit helps us tell others about Jesus**— *Acts 1:8*

Model & Practice: Pray with your disciple, asking the Holy Spirit to fill you and to take control of your life. Encourage your disciple to do the same.

Action Step: Begin each day asking the Holy Spirit to fill you and take control of your life. You may need to ask Him to fill you multiple times throughout the day.

Chapter 2– My Story

Every disciple maker will share their story of how Jesus changed their life.

Your Story is unique and a powerful way to tell others about Jesus. Usually a story has three parts:
1. How was my life like before I believed in Christ
2. How I came to know Christ
3. How my life has changed after knowing Christ

Key Principle: Every believer is a disciple, and every disciple is called to be a disciple maker.

Key Scriptures:

1. **Every believer is called to make disciples—**
   Matthew 28:19-20

2. **Every believer is called to love God and love others—**
   Matthew 22:34-40

Model & Practice: Tell your story and let your disciples practice telling their story. Help as needed.

Action Step: Share your story with one person on your list or a Pre-Christian this week.

Chapter 3– God's Story

Every disciple maker will make disciples by telling God's story.

God's Story is sometimes called the Gospel. It tells how to have a relationship with God through His Son, Jesus.

Key Principle: God loved the world so much that He sent His Son Jesus, so that those who believe in Him will receive eternal life *(John 3:16)*.

Key Scriptures:

1. *Romans 3:23, "for all have sinned and fall short of the glory of God."*
2. *Romans 5:8, "But God demonstrates His own love toward us, in that while we were still sinners, Christ died for us."*
3. *Romans 10:9, "...if you confess with your mouth the Lord Jesus and believe in your heart that God raised Him from the dead, you will be saved."*

Model & Practice: Tell God's story using 3 Circles. Next, listen to your disciple practice telling God's story and help as needed.

Action Step: Tell God's Story with one person on your list or with a Pre-Christian.

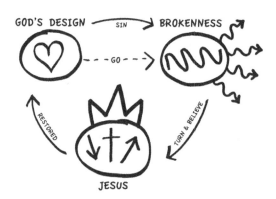

Chapter 4– Your Assurance of Salvation

Every disciple maker will stand firm in the assurance of their salvation and help others do the same.

Key Principle: If you have trusted Jesus to be your Savior and Lord, then you have received eternal life! You are Kingdom Citizen! Your service to the King starts here and now!

Key Scriptures:

1. **The path to eternal life is through Jesus**— *1 John 5:11-13*

2. **Faith in Jesus is the way of salvation**— *John 14:6*

3. **Your new identity**— *2 Corinthians 5:17*

4. **Your assurance of salvation**— *1 John 1:7-9*

Model & Practice: Go through the Key Scriptures and encourage your new believer that they can be confident in the assurance of their salvation.

Action Step: Try to memorize at least one of the Key Scriptures.

Chapter 5– Living a Life of Prayer

Every disciple maker will experience a healthy prayer life in tune with the Holy Spirit.

Prayer is "talking" with God, "listening" to God, and "hearing" from God. Jesus gave a simple example to follow when we pray.

Key Principle: Listen and talk to God throughout the day— *1 Thessalonians 5: 16-18*

Key Scripture: The Lord's Prayer-*Matthew 6:9-13*

1. **Talk to God like a Father (or daddy)**— *Matthew 6:9*
2. **Worship and praise Him**— *Matthew 6:9*
3. **Pray for Jesus to set the world right and return soon**— *Matthew 6:10*
4. **Focus on advancing His Kingdom**— *Matthew 6:10*
5. **Ask Him to lead and be Master of your life**— *Matthew 6:10*
6. **Ask Him to meet your needs and those of others you know**—*Matthew 6:11*
7. **Confess your sins to Him and forgive those you have not forgiven**— *Matthew 6:12*
8. **Ask Him for protection and victory over temptation and sin**— *Matthew 6:13*

Model & Practice: Pray the Lord's prayer together.

Action Step: Pray the Lord's prayer 7 minutes a day, 7 days a week, for 7 people.

Chapter 6— Daily Devotions

Every disciple maker will experience God through daily devotions.

To really know a person, you need to have regular contact. If you want to have a close relationship with God, it is helpful to set a time **just for God** each day—this is called daily devotions.

Key Principle: The main purpose of daily devotions is to know and worship God and respond in obedience to what His Word and Spirit say.

Key Scriptures:

1. **Pursue God as a priority in your life**— *Matthew 6:33*

2. **Trust in God and rely on Him to lead you**— *Proverbs 3:5-6*

Model & Practice: Model how you do your own daily devotions. Encourage your disciple to do the same.

Action Step: Identify a consistent and specific time and place for daily devotions. Who will keep you accountable? Download the YouVersion Bible App and identify a Bible reading plan.

Chapter 7– Learning to Feed Yourself

Every disciple maker will live a life committed to intentional, obedient, and personal Bible study.

A newborn baby relies on his mother to be fed, but must eventually learn to feed himself. In the same way, a Christian must learn to feed themselves. This can be done through personal Bible study.

Key Principle & Scripture: Every believer must learn to grow in their understanding, trusting, and obeying of God's Word—*2 Timothy 3:16*

Model & Practice: Practice together the personal Bible study method with your disciple (Reference Chapter 7 for full instructions). In four sections note: Scripture, My Own Words, I Will, and Prayer & Share.

1. **SCRIPTURE:** copy the passage word-for-word exactly how it is written in the Bible.
2. **MY OWN WORDS:** rewrite the passage in your own words.
3. **I COMMIT TO:** ask the Holy Spirit to reveal things you need to add to your life, take away from your life, or change in your life to obey this passage. **Be specific!**
4. **PRAYER & SHARE:** Prayerfully reflect on who needs to hear the truths God has revealed to you. Share your 'I Will' statements and hold each other accountable. Look for opportunities to share what God said with others.

Action Step: Each day practice the Personal Bible Study method. Follow through with all of your "I Will" statements, and share with one person on your list or a pre-Christian.

Chapter 8—God Our Heavenly Father

Every disciple maker will experience and share with others the blessings of God as Heavenly Father.

Key Principle: God is your Heavenly Father and loves you unconditionally.

Key Scriptures:

1. **Our Heavenly Father Loves**— *Romans 5:8*

2. **Our Heavenly Father Protects**— *2 Kings 6:15-18*

3. **Our Heavenly Father Provides**— *Philippians 4:19*

4. **Our Heavenly Father Disciplines**— *Hebrews 12:6-7*

Model & Practice: Identify one way you can show love to your disciples this week. Pray with them and encourage them from the Key Scriptures.

Action Step: Share about your Heavenly Father and His love to one person on your list or a pre-Christian this week.

Chapter 9– Life in the Church

Every disciple maker will be part of a local body of believers committed to the purposes of Christ and His Church.

Key Principle: A spiritual family— with Christ in their midst as King— who love God, love others, and multiply disciples.

Key Scriptures:

1. Baptism is commanded by Jesus and is how we go public with our faith *(Matthew 28:19-20, Romans 6:1-14, Acts 2:41)*.

2. The Lord's Supper (Communion) is commanded by Jesus and is how we celebrate and remember His sacrifice *(Matthew 26:17-19, 26-30)*.

3. Sacrificial giving is one way we show love and obedience to Jesus' command to love God & love others *(Acts 2:42-47, 2 Corinthians 9:7)*.

Model & Practice: Evaluate and discuss together the growth, development, and progress of your disciples. Consider the fruit that is evidenced in their life and how they can better grow in their walk with Christ.

Action Step: Join a local body of believers, experience baptism if you have not already been baptized. Begin or continue taking the Lord's Supper and giving.

59467752R00075

Made in the USA
Columbia, SC
06 June 2019